Fires of Heaven

Fires of Heaven

poems of faith & sense by

James B. Nicola

Shanti Arts Publishing
Brunswick, Maine

Fires of Heaven
poems of faith & sense

Copyright © 2020 James B. Nicola

All Rights Reserved
No part of this book may be used or reproduced in any manner whatsoever without written permission from the publisher except in the case of brief quotations embodied in critical articles and reviews.

Published by Shanti Arts Publishing
Interior and cover design by Shanti Arts Designs

Shanti Arts LLC | 193 Hillside Road
Brunswick, Maine 04011 | shantiarts.com

Cover: William Blake, *Jerusalem, Plate 35*, "Then the Divine hand....", 1804–1820. Relief etching printed in orange with pen and black ink and watercolor on moderately thick, smooth, cream wove paper. 8.85 x 6.49 inches (22.5 x 16.5 cm). Yale Center for British Art, New Haven, Connecticut. Public domain. Wikimedia Commons.

Notes: (1) Untitled poems are identified by opening lines or phrases and not capitalized as titles would be. (2) Multiple blank lines in some poems are intentional. (3) A single blank line is lost due to pagination between pages 24-25, 30-31, 36-37, 42-43, 48-49, 53-54, 54-55, 72-73, and 133-134. All other page turns occur mid-stanza or between clearly indicated sections.

No actual person, living or dead, should be construed as represented in these poems except where mentioned expressly by name.

Printed in the United States of America

ISBN: 978-1-951651-45-9 (softcover)

Library of Congress Control Number: 2020950741

*To those who've had the passing thought
That even thought can be divine*

*And those who haven't had the thought
Till now*

Also by James B. Nicola

— poetry —

Quickening:
Poems from Before and Beyond

Out of Nothing:
Poems of Art and Artists

Wind in the Cave

Stage to Page:
Poems from the Theater

Manhattan Plaza

— non-fiction —

Playing the Audience:
The Practical Actor's Guide to Live Performance

Man lives, Gods die:
It is only the genuflection that survives.
                    —Padraic Fallon

I know as well as the next man that faith,
Some measure of faith, is needed by us all.
Pure doubt is death.
                    —Robert Francis

Contents

Alternate Perspectives	15
Heraclitus	16
Choosing	17
If each star	18
The Moment in a Service	19
Kinds	20
If you think you see God by day	21
The Process of Water	22
Blade	23
Aurora	24
So, The Modern	26
Shortcoming	27
Proving, An Apologia	28
Apostrophe	30
Acts of Creation	32
Checking	33
More than a Dream	34
One Day Years Ago	36
One Day in a Cave	38
After Eve	39
Above and Below	40
Beatitudes and Bravery	41
Hellsgate	42
The Invention of Mephistopheles	44
Mixed Praise	45
The Power of Belief	46
Hell	47
Cross-Examination	48
Confusion 1	50
When they spun	51
Prophets and Poets	52
The Belfry	53
One time, in the middle	56
Crèche	58
Cathedrals	59

Religion 1: The teller emerges	60
Thriller	61
Awe 2	62
Green	63
The Birth of Capitalism	64
Spire	67
marmorata	68
Chess and the Master	70
Workshop Vision	71
The Margin of Error	72
The Evangelist	74
Bridge	75
Sunday School	76
Grammar Lesson	78
Buttress	80
Apples	81
Desert-Ambling, or, The Beauty Part	82
"Moses"	83
Interpretation	84
Gothic	85
Four Realms	86
David and Absalom	87
Oil Can	88
Lamp Stand	89
Patty Cake	92
God's Love	93
I am Not That I Am	94
Divinity, or, Man	95
Collection Basket	96
Bakers	97
Nature Walk	98
Chimes	99
Potential	100
Few	101
Easter 2003, A True Story	102
Religion 2: Not to Say	104

Bright Eye	105
When the Collection Dish Comes Round	106
Feather and Flame	108
Back Room	109
The Parson	110
"The Creation of Adam"	111
At the Center	112
Circle and Cross	113
Out with Bacchus	114
Lesson from the Master	115
The Reformed	116
The Histories, Back When	117
Religion 3: He stood draped	118
Night Sky	119
Heaven, Whateveritis	120
Saturdays	121
Fear and Faith, An Interview	122
Organs	123
Holidays	124
Revisions	125
The Exercise of Reason	126
Postcard from *Republicca*	127
The Outlaw	128
Were He to think of sky	129
Feathers 2	130
Glad	131
Exegesis on a Church Sign	132
A Certain Faith	136
And all that All	138
Litany	139
Face to Face, A True Story	140
The Moment	141
Not What You Might Think	142
To Help You Think	143

Alternate Perspectives

For instance, that a graveyard is a garden
too, which, though seeming still, careers through space
on a great round spheroid ship squashed in at poles
with flaws, dents, bumps, like an uncultured pearl,
a natural jewel. And when a soul's turned in
it fertilizes futures with more carbon
and sand to make more pearl, emerald, diamond.

Or that Earth's but a blue-green stud, a bauble,
presumed to be cherished by Someone Who
keeps us in His curio box. And if He
has gotten at least one ear pieced, that we
might be heard—or, if plugged into His navel,
be warmed by an abdomen's circulation,
digestion, breathing, pulses of a heart. . . .

Heraclitus

He said that of the four, Fire
was first, the font of Everything,
though he too looked around and saw

only Earth, Water and Air: that is,
Solid, Liquid and Gas;
Fire being ephemeral, and rare.

He had no microscope back then.
Who taught him how to look and know
the furnace inside every atom

ablaze with energy
inextinguishable?
That even crystal, ice and diamond,

were far more hot than cold
just in their being there?
That fire was

the word
Yes
to almost everything?

Someone
must have given him
The Word!

And if In the beginning was the Word,
The Word was Yes,
and Yes was Fire.

Choosing

Choosing to live is to acknowledge God;
doing it without knowing, this is faith—
especially now that you've realized
that you don't have to. There's no greater act—
not all the exegeses, prayers, nor oaths—
than living. All else is but conjugation
and punctuation that convey what is
already, in the mere quotidian:

the blade of grass, a starlit sky, the bee,
the wind-whirled plastic bag, or you-and-me.
I don't pretend that any of these are
God, but that through us you might hear His Voice
or catch a glimpse, in the case of a star,
of the Unseen. The rest, my dear, is choice.

If each star

If each star
were a Soul
that might explain a lot—
but no matter,
for each certainly
acts
as if it were.

And if there
were a God
it might explain a lot—
like all matter;
so we, certainly,
act
as if there were,

notwithstanding
the indefinableness
of the terms
above.

The Moment in a Service

The moment
in a service
when,
lately,

the priest or minister
parson or preacher
asks you to turn to someone behind you
or reach for someone who's turned to you
and shake their hand and say something like
Peace be with you

makes me rethink the value of kid gloves
and of roped-off, rich-clan pews
and of other less expensive ways
of avoiding the triumph of germs

like making a fist and chucking you sidewise
on an unsuspecting elbow
or grabbing your neck
in a brotherly elbow lock.

Of course instead of *Peace* I might say
Hey buddy, or
Great to see you, or maybe even
How's it hanging?

and one day
I will dare to do
just that

and someone
will suspect me
at last
of being sincere.

Kinds

There are so many varieties
of fruits and mushrooms safe to chew,
of plants with flowers wrought to please
the eye and nose of birds and bees—
that happen to please persons', too!—
that sometimes I can see how you
might think there's what you call "Divine
Intelligence" in the design.

I can even recall the time
as a child that I first tasted lime.
Refreshed, I thought, no, felt, no, knew,
no, actually swallowed, The Sublime.
And after all the world had been
almost as fine with only lemon:
The choice could only have been due
to God, I guessed. But then I grew

and tasted all the marques of wine,
the Mogen David and the fine,
decanted both to please and sell,
so any "believer" might just as well
have called the Supreme Intelligence
a Vintner, Marketer, Inventor,
The One That Makes The Difference.
Choosing your poor moniker
forsakes the Heart for the Brain, or Mind.
His Work is brilliantly designed
but may not be more wise than kind—
which the child in me still learns, I suppose,
time after time after time after time
from every mushroom, lemon, lime
and rose.

If you think you see God by day

If you think you see God by day
it might
be merely light.
But if you spot a deity
at night
you must be right!

The Process of Water

When Shirley MacLaine
or someone like that
says she is
or rather has
god in her or
something like that
it means she is as a drop
dropped on the ocean
there being of course
many other
drops.

A sea's aloof from neither river nor rain,
but welcomes
and salts all
drop by drop
till we are born—
evaporate—
condense with experience—
then fall—
and return
as rain.

And everyone and everything
alive or once alive or soon alive
is as a drop
in that water process
to be bathed in or drunk
by the eternal thirst
of Earth, of us, of
the ocean god
or someone
somewhere
somewhat, I think,
like that.

Blade

Like a slash of virgin grass
in a green communal ignorance

proud, pointed, reaching up
slicing toward an azure or albion or
ashen or effervescent ebony beyond

through a nothing light as any unhummed air

caressed—no kissed—by what must be
the gusto of a mere breath, I

know no puff-cheeked cherub imp exhaled
nor windgod bellowed angrily or bored

but cannot help but
feel
and want to bow:

as a Man
of bone and fist
I'm unable to, and

tremble;

but as a Mind
I imagine my soul
supine on the lawn

and every now and then
wake up just so
amazed and renewed

by that
imagination's
conquest

Aurora

The day you proved to me that the same steps
of the fire dance—cool, multicolored flames—
only upside-down, are danced at the same time
at the southern pole, is when I began
to lose my faith, then my ability
to create or recreate, then care enough
to dance or love or fight about anything.
Was none of heaven wild enough to stay
inscrutable? Was all awe to be parsed?

I used to look up, on those rare cold nights,
and see silent teams of opposing hues and cries
engage with all the turbulence of childhood's
inner moods. I'd imagine a pantheon
of demi-deities, preparing for
love—trying to reach out, embrace, or spoon—
or for war—clenched, with great gleaming scimitars
in hand—dazzling like eager, messy, prisms.
Perhaps they celebrated not a prologue,
but the aftermath—of battle, consummation,
or the far more festive fervor of creation.

Now I have turned my focus in the other
direction. I don't know Who suggested
I do, but can't not-knowing be better?
I look not with the eyes, not quite the mind,
but with the heart, upward yet inward, at
the hewing hues, the din of deafening silence,
the storm of peace, the harmless violence,
the uncontrolled control, lights preening, primping,
strutting, showing off their gaudy garments,
the inscrutable splendor of the dark.

Memory being portable, contained
inside, all the brilliant loving fury
of those select Alaskan nights,
unchained in its ignorance,
goes with me everywhere,
summoned at will
or of its own accord. It rises
like an unseen tide on an unknown world's dark side.
When it comes, I stay up all night—
eyes closed, eyes open, it doesn't matter.
And as long as the colors dance or fight,
or crave to love,
I persist,
grateful for the dervishes' celestial scimitars.
And I suspect, with their night's entertainment,
the dark unpredictable, intimate,
that between the Earth's antipodes—
the anodes of the Great Battery—
there must exist
a cause or soul worth dueling for,
or dancing for,
engaging with,
waiting only
for me to stumble upon it
some day
to enlighten
the cold, faithless night.

So, The Modern

When I call the sky, the ocean, the world, Life
or Being itself—when I call these my Teachers,
you call me on it and say that that's a lie
in that it's a metaphor. Nature does not want
to teach, but is, and wants only to continue—
But even that is imputing human desire
to the senseless sense of nature. This is much
like how we find an aim in modern art.
But to tell plain truth one can't use metaphor.

For if the facts are: I have learned so much
from looking at and flying in the sky,
from sailing on and swimming in the sea,
as from breathing in, walking on, growing up from the earth,
splendificating nature as my world,
it is also so that none of these teachers gave
a whit whether I learned a thing or not,
only that I continue—But even that
is something I can only hope is So.

Well so it is with a contemporary painting
or sculpture, or poem, or dance, or piece of music.
What it wants to be, what I want it to be,
more than it is, that is—is what I impute
to it, not what is necessarily there.
Of course I'd be hard pressed to say that jazz
or the jitterbug is sad. No, they simply must
have been born from joy, as Munch's *Scream* must
have been shrieked, at least the first time, from raw anguish.
(Later, of course, from remembrance of that sound.)

So Nature's wellspring and purpose has to be—
Well, whatever you say, Sir, in the end.

And God must be a modern after all.

Shortcoming

I have a shortcoming that
makes me a nasty, ungrateful creature,
I know.
My gifts abound
and I have so much to be thankful for,
and *All that breathes is holy*, yes I know,
but I have some limits.

One, the slug.
Two, the cockroach.
Add to this the tsetse fly.
Then Hitler, and the like.

They cannot be indulged
as Adam and Eve did the Serpent,
who, after all, was but an instrument
voicing the will of God.

The critters on this list, though—
I cannot believe they are
from God at all, although I know it's so.
And so I squash them—or wish that I could—
worse, am unbothered by this shortcoming.

Proving, An Apologia

One can and has devised a million kinds
of proof, but with my own of God, I can
never go back to the pre-proven mind.
For with the proving comes intransigence
as sudden as the shutters of a house
flapping—. I can't decide: open or shut?
But that they'll have to stay this way forever,
this new way, I suspect so strongly that—

An entrance seems to loom, which I'm to make,
but which way the procession, in or out,
remains unclear: I tend both toward the world
and into a seclusion. Strange. And now
with the new armor, confidence and truth
I've come upon, worked toward, was bestowed
with no relation to the awful work
and no regard for changes it requires,
I ponder post-proof obligations, thus:

If to dwell in the house, is it a warm
inviting one, or am I sealed in tight?
If out among my brethren, how to go:
as hero or as outcast; leader, fool;
shouting wisdom, or acting wise, but mute?
Sociological discrepancies
like these support no proofs; I've found no facts
or precedents to help me figure out
the rites of what to do, or say, or be.

So though I stand as strong as granite stone
I flow in waves like oceans pied with jellies
the unsuspecting swimmer comes upon
from time to time. I've started to suspect

it matters little if I shout (or write)
hermetically of esoterica
nor whether I'm within the house or out;
nor whether anyone but you hears me
at all. All matters little, except that
the house is not still: worlds are not compact,
but metamorphose in this quiet rapture,
which, wherever I breathe and go, expands,
daily growing larger, as I am.

Apostrophe

Since matter now is energy
    so then might an existence be
a Great One's great apostrophe:

for you He'd be addressing you,
    for me, me. You might wonder Who
is wondering—I wonder too

Who's fraught with such a whimsy'd will
    that in conjecture He'd instill
in gentle kind the urge to kill;

in virtue, vanity and vice;
    toss in temptation to entice
the transformation in a trice

from good to bad, to war from peace.
    Do warring sentiments increase
as some Creator's rash caprice

no deeper than a passing thought
    in which the passing person's caught
and helpless, so we cannot not?—

existence swirling in the space
    between nerve ends behind the face
of our capricious master race

whose thought's as sudden as a spark
    from end to end, from quark to quark
like lightning, lightening the dark?

I've studied and so far can't find
    a theory better than our kind
existing in an Other's mind

Who's far more like a man than God,
    so wicked, or at least so flawed,
or—this you must admit—so odd!

Still, theories rise from ignorance,—
    I've truly no idea whence
peace, love, and wickedness commence

as thought's but focused attitude,
    exploiting unearned latitude,
awaiting a beatitude . . .

Acts of Creation

A difference between man and mighty God—
The One Who's introduced in Genesis—
Is: Man alone can't see if his is *good*,
The fruit of his creative energies.
He needs opinion, or posterity:
Widespread approval of his eager claim
To greatness: one shrewd critic's nodding eye
Inspiring immortality, or fame.

A man laced with Integrity, though, knows
Techniques of looking at what he's put down
With fresh eyes; he is eager to expose
The weak parts, then revises, when alone.
Oh, since that first day's letting of the light,
Has God been working, too, on a rewrite?

Checking

The baker clicks the oven light and peeks
The carpenter plops his level down and squints

The poodle tours the upstairs hall and sniffs
The parent tips the crib with an airblown kiss

The pilot rereads the dials on his dash
    particularly during or before a storm

The poet peers *out* a familiar window
The familiar, like a guardian angel, *in*

But God, or gods
    that some have forged
    and puffed beyond the clouds

        must be

            caught
                in the middle
                    of a blink

More than a Dream

1. A dream?

Part of me went away awhile.
    The rest of me stayed here
and, stumbling on a gilded hall
    where greatness should appear,

I waited for it to descend—
    Him, if you will, or Her—
preceded by a Them, the band
    incensed in herbs and myrrh

who played, but whom we could not hear,
    just felt, their trumpets blown
in silent blasts that rode the air.
    The next segment outshone

the previous one, and on and on
    until the climax came.
I shivered so to look upon
    a face I could not name.

Then all about began to change,
    transforming quietly,
so hot and bright yet calm, a strange
    earth-passion flowed through me,

forbade me looking at the star.
    Though one part wanted to,
the rest decided to defer.
    And then I woke, to You.

2.   Not a dream

I trembled, teary-eyed, and laughed;
    then, in the mirror, saw
a glow of fire, cool and soft,
    like love contained by awe.

Friends said they saw a mystic wash
    of rose across my face
as if a dove or burning bush
    had smitten me with Grace.

I loved my fellow man that week—
    and woman, too, and all,
both seen and unseen. But that week
    went by, as spring to fall.

3.   More than a dream

I wrote so I would not forget,
    though, what befell me then
and live remembering, in wait
    for You to come again.

One Day Years Ago

When someone said that we, or you, or I
were made in His image, this someone did
not mean a simulacrum of, well, Him;
rather, an idea He entertained
that entertained Him, one day, years ago

as a child might make a castle of the sand
on a beach and watch it, or not watch it, go;
or an emperor build a city; an artist
or architect, a masterpiece; a thinker,
scribbles of dreamt-on verse, from time to Time.

Of course, with *stanzas*, verse becomes a house
of *rooms*, and with a book of verse, a city;
with several books, an empire might be born,
far-sprawling, then forgotten. That is why

I loved discovering on the beach, one day
years ago, the old man who told me he
had been a poet, and loved helping him
concoct a castle and watch the gentle waves
of a lazy rising afternoon tide wash
it over so it glistened in the foam
until, by dusk, all three of us were gone.

I now wish I had asked the man his name
so that today I might track down a volume
of him, and images he had one day
years ago, worthy of creation, then.

The thought of him still haunts me as an im-
age, though, of the sands at St. Augustine,
where I played in the sand, once, years ago:
particularly when I'm on a foam-
washed beach, with children playing, some old man,
and me, and not a castle's to be seen,
and the gentle rote makes every sand-grain glisten.

One Day in a Cave

Under a cave's dank eaves I found the trace
of Someone's presence: runes etched in the stone
and moss, illuminating that thick place
like a black forest, where I walked alone

one day in blithe abandon: then the Face
of their Author, dappled light diffused in dew,
like morning—Scripture, natural as grace,
be-lettered in a tongue I only knew

through feeling. And I could not fathom how.
Since that day, every line is less a Mys-
tery with every upward look or way-
ward revelation. Caves are nested now,
the night sky but one vault in a nexus
of caves, all bright and numberless as day.

After Eve

The human race at last, after Eve
and Adam loved each other and raced
the hell out of there, began to love
in an adult way. A soft hello
would turn into a passion in a
millisecond. A silent, slow turn
of the head, a wink, then a second
hello—brought another wink, a smile,
two smiles, then closeness, and another
world, planets coming closer, closer,
and on the horizon, a third world
emerging from their rumble, their rise
to night, after nightfall, as they'd merge,
maybe clasping each other all night,
as Eve and Adam never could clasp
until their fall, as we this evening
have met, faced each other, turned, fallen
into the darkness that births each life
here, after eve, at last, in the dark.

Above and Below

If Heaven lies above and Hell below
(as many still imagine and depict
who see the sun, then note the downward flow
of lava), there's a wicked majesty
(if not quite wicked, surely derelict)
when devil-thunders roar and death-winds blow
and lightning cracks a law-abiding tree
or slays a good man. Yet while skies inflict,
the Earth (soil, sunshine, rain) makes all things grow
with her earth-goddess personality.
Such evidences wholly contradict
the old-school celestial geography—
Are Hell and Heaven—One? I wonder . . . (though
suspect we're really not supposed to know).

Beatitudes and Bravery

With them there came, I felt, a duty to
report them, some day. This task would require
a certain boldness altogether new

to me. I have to write this, then. I do
not want to, but we serve a purpose higher,
with which there comes, I feel, the duty to

describe one, if I can. To whom, though? You?
Imagine being lit then by a fire
of certain boldness, altogether new.

As sudden as a sledgehammer swung through
me—gently as a cherub-tickled lyre,
though—all at once I felt the duty to

report how all I ever thought I knew,
I didn't—only felt, like young desire,
whose certain boldness, altogether new,

inspires me to tell what I know is true.
Or was. Once. Soon. For now, let me retire
awhile, and contemplate my duty to
uncertain boldness, altogether new.

Hellsgate

I once saw a huge head of Hellsgate
in a picture book called Olde Folk Tales.
    The opposite page
      showed the rest of the stage
of a mummers' play touring through Wales.

The face of the head was all twisted
and mottled with sores, warts and moles
    and the biggest damn maw
      you ever saw
hungry for passing souls

from the back of the pub, or the tar pits,
or the next- or the next-to-next town,
    down which you would be sent
      if you didn't repent.
And it looked like a long way down.

❖

Since then, I've seen myriad movies
full of horror, vice, grossness and gore
    where the portal to hell
      was a myth to dispel
only to visit once more.

One night in the rear of a tavern
patrons quite unabashedly chattered
    about stealing and cheating
      on taxes and beating
their wives as if none of it mattered.

Then I saw on the back door a door plaque
with a hells-mouth from which rose a laughter
    so piercing and scar-
        y I raced out of there.
I keep hearing it, though, decades after.

The Invention of Mephistopheles

My invention, Mephistopheles,
was a fairy story simply spun
to while away the centuries
and attract pure souls of children

who have not yet attained the age
that thirsts for more abstracted sin.
For I was born to grace the stage:
not haunt you from within,

but entertain, as snakes were sent
to play with Adam and Eve.
(By the way, their talking serpent,
notwithstanding what you believe,

was not me. That I flat out deny.
Me, pose as a talking creature?
Bah. Who says I would, tells a devil's lie.
It's not in my humanist nature;

rather, I'm in yours. The part you should,
you show your friends and family,
keeping the part that poses as good
from the real you, made from me.)

As children, through my fairy tales,
give their darker sides existence
with tails, a trident, fireballs
and other hot props for assistance,

so I am born. From mischief, sure,
but more from divine incentive—
for you to divide, appearing pure—
oh so devilishly inventive.

Mixed Praise

If God makes deluges *and* droughts,
I don't think I can fathom God.
Is He unbalanced, is He unwell,
cursing with plenty, blessing with less
than enough? How can I, starving, bless
the feast? Alas, I'm stolider than
that, or smarter, or stupider,
to pretend that Nothing is a feast.
    And in your absence I cannot pretend.

If God's The One Who makes you absent,
what the h--- is He, that I
should glorify? Pray? I would, sure,
except I don't dare make a sound
for fear of cursing, for which I'd
be damned, and apart from you forever.
But then you return, and I'm insane
with joy. And no hunger, drought,
    or deluge can make me not praise God.

The Power of Belief

Be careful what you say, where, and to whom.
To talk about enlightened things to some
new friends at a fried chicken restaurant
in a state you're visiting is fine, but don't
be tempted, in a rush, to speak too loud
to your table-mates unless you know the crowd.

You know beliefs are "myths more true than fact,"
but some believe what they believe's exactly
true, and even murder is no sin
but their responsibility when in
the presence of the devil, which is you,
no matter that you know it isn't true.

In any time zone, any latitude
where people have endured, the attitude
endures. The ecumenical is not
welcomed, nor an elucidating thought
allowed. In my experience the danger
is most acute wherever you're the stranger.

How is it, you have asked, that I can know
about so many places? Did I go
all over the world to teach an enlightened
philosophy, to be, at each place, frightened?
But I am not the point. O, friend! Think harder
when you are tempted, too, to play the martyr.

Hell

If Hell is where the other guy is headed:
where he gets to dress up for Hallowe'en
and scare survivors daily, and be dreaded
and feared; and where he never has to mean
what he says; where there are no consequences
for lying; where he's not required to sing
on key, or worry about mending fences,
or burning bridges—about anything,
in fact; and where, even if he'd been wedded
in life, it wouldn't matter, he could do
whatever with whomever, any way
and as often as he'd want—and without you;
and if it's where the other *gal* is headed
as well: I'd like to visit there, some day.

Cross-Examination

"If you can say
     I love you
now
and mean it
then I believe in God."

This said I to an adversary
when I was on the stand
under oath.

He called me an idiot,
so I
went on:

"Religion may be
an excuse for idiocy and faith,
Faith, an excuse
for idiocy and religion,

"but if you can say
     I love you
or even think it,

"then
there's
God."

Now,
whether he said *I love you*
or not didn't matter.
He thought it, and could:

But God was not dependent on
our words, or acts,
or thoughts,

or feelings,
or degree of
sincerity:

Only on Is-ness itself

Which we confirm by *If,*
Love
I, and
You.

And even today,
not only can I believe
but know
It is.

Confusion 1

I was confused, then, when I believed all
that I was told, that Darkness was the Foe,
and not what made, but what opposed, the soul.

When I saw the fallacy of the Fall,
however, then I knew I didn't know.
I'd been confused, then, when I believed all

that I was told. The arrogance—the gall—
of men in robes to say what was not so;
that my knowledge was what opposed the soul.

Yet some thought themselves—good men, telling tall
tales. Who was I to tell them where to go?
(But I had been confused, when I believed all

those stories.) Dark *makes* light; it is the wall
of the garden wherein universes grow!
And this knowledge does not oppose the soul,

any more than love and sex, Bacchus and Baal,
or the Serpent, are purveyors of woe.
No, we were confused when we believed all
that was—was made—was what opposed the soul.

When they spun

When they spun
The Story
Later
They made it
The Night that
The Animals

Talked.

But I should hope
It was rather
The Night that
The Humans

Didn't.

Prophets and Poets

What's said and noted, some manipulate;
what's unsaid, though, no mortal hand can touch.
So prophets speak but never do notate;
what poets scratch is seldom noted much.

But utterances are far from everything;
their records, babes born under a new moon,
orphaned forever, and yet born to sing,
if only someone could recall the tune.

When Scripture's poetry, a truth is wrung,
because the meaning's not the melody's
harangue, twisted, dripped dry. It's the unsung,
the unsaid, teeming with ambiguities,
wherein one can shy short of blasphemies.
The distinction's yours to make. Thank God you're young.

The Belfry

When I was small
white pigeons
lived up there.

He'd let me climb up
to watch the big bell
ring during service

and they'd coo and bill
unmoved until
he pulled on the giant cord

below. Then they'd flap
and flutter and fly
and come back. And not

infrequently a dove
would land on my shoulder.
(After they had gotten to know me,

that is, after weeks, months, years
of faithful Sundays.)
He's old now

but still the sacristan
although the chimes
are prerecorded.

At his wife's funeral
I went back.
He told me that

—continued

the doves had left.
Next day I rang
and made him let me up.

It was true, the doves
were gone, the bell,
much smaller, was tied off,

and had a big old crack,
and everything in the belfry
was covered

with crusting
guano.
I stood there awhile,

breathless.
(It was some
climb.)

When I sat on the square
below the tower
to eat my lunch

a flock of unexpected pigeons
flew down and
joined me.

One
hopped up
on my bench

and enjoyed a crust
from my hand. I said
out loud to it

What happened to you?
and it looked up, as if
it had heard

and was
asking me
the same.

One time, in the middle

One time, in the middle of a foreign city,
I came upon, quite unexpectedly,
a quaint cathedral in a busy square.
I crept in and waddled down the aisle
between the rows of nearly empty seats
erected for a multitude not there
and as I arrived in front, as the vault
of the transept was higher than that of the aisle,
it seemed that in my lowly quiet
I, too, began to rise. Impressed
by the work of man, then,
and my experience of it, now,
I suddenly dropped
unintentionally
to my knees.

One time, touring on a bike in Normandy,
I came upon—and quite expectedly,
this time—a city of the dead
and a sea of markers: white crosses and stars
rising from the emerald of new-mown grass,
from me all the way to the horizon.
I dismounted the rented bike and paced a lane
between the rows of clean,
perfect, nearly uniform tombstones and,
overwhelmed by the work and presence
of man, both then and now,
and my experience of it,
I suddenly dropped
unintentionally
to my knees.

One time, in a mountain village,
after a rain, but unexpectedly,
a triple rainbow in the late blue sky
appeared. The multitude emerged
from shops and homes to the street
and was looking upward, as an unformed,
impromptu, gladly inconvenienced congregation,
their faces bathed by the lowering sun.
Suddenly aware of the presence
and work of someone other than man,
convulsing in a strange new joy,
wet from the rain-kissed ground as well as from
the joyous oil of tears that fell,
my soul dropped down, unintentionally,
to my knees, then on all fours, and finally
prostrate on the ground
as if in supplication
but with nothing more I could think of
to ask for.

Crèche

You should have seen the Christmas crèche
inside our parish church.
I paid a buck and made a wish
under the chapel arch

then lit a votive candle. They
had placed twelve dozen an-
imals around the holly and hay,
and there were three wise men,

Mary, Joseph, and a cradle—
you know the layout, then?
I felt right in the middle
of the story and the scene.

Then someone must have flicked an ash—
in spite of the big red sign—
and lit a straw, 'cause in a flash
the church and crèche were gone.

The hay had been dry since August, and
the figures were all wood,
as if some Mastermind had planned
the end of them for good.

Our parish had no funds to call
upon, but we learned to pray
by the sooty stones of a fallen wall
and kneel on soggy hay.

Cathedrals

Humble and grand. The feeling: when they're shut,
they're open, when the builders get them right.
The cosmic rainbow filtered from without
to half man-made, half beatific light.

Reflection. Round the ambulatory
bedapplements that bathe the wood, the crowd,
the stone, their stillness echoed from a story
where no soul living ever is allowed.

Incense. Some people take a pew. Some pray.
Some kneel, breathe in, and sigh. I stroll instead—
and hear some god or demigod of Form
say, Stop. Look up. Now. Put the pen away.
I hear and sit, look up, then dip my head,
the hollowness grown huge, and cold, and warm.

Religion 1: The teller emerges

The teller emerges from a dark back
room. It feels I've waited at the window
to have Mine weighed longer than necessary.
And then she overcharges. And I gripe,
figure I'll take my business elsewhere, but
as if she's read my mind she says THERE IS
NO ELSEWHERE. STAND ASIDE. I stand aside
and note that she's a he. They work in shifts,
epicene, in black, or white, or cloaked
in seasonal colors, but all attractive
in some way, all emerging from a room
too dark to see inside. And as a world
of customers have Theirs weighed, I soon see
how the tellers sneak a thumb on the scale,
like a greengrocer in a foreign land who knows
you'll never see them again, and won't complain.
So all of us are overcharged. A spark
of shock in each face registers the price
but we gird and gild ourselves, and one
by one pass to an inner room to gather
in various hordes at sundry gates and wait
for a ferry, a plane, a doomed dirigible.

Thriller

I been collectin clues here right along, but for the life of me I can't
>figure which *are* clues and which are those red herrings.
>Geezus, He's clever.

Forensic evidence? Sure, kid: there're traces everywhere, like
>fingerprints, but not. And DNA? Yeah, loads, but, so? In
>this case DNA don't really help.

The mindset and the M.O. of the Perpetrator has been heavily
>profiled. Here lookit all these files. Take 'em.

And we got us a composite sketch done up by an artist from the
>witnesses' reports. But ya gotta admit, they have either
>been kinda crazy, or unreliable, or otherwise discredited.

But I gotta be gettin close, with all this crap piled up around me,
>stacked on shelves and tables and smotherin the floor with
>trails and leads. I must be onto Him, 'cuz why else would
>He have sent goons with first the flood and then the fire?

If only I could get one good eye-witness.

Say! Maybe I could go over there myself. I'll tie a string and leave
>one end with you, so that when I see the face of
>Whodunit I'll tug on mine to signal, in Morse Code—ya
>know it? But if anything happens to me, kid, that means ya
>gotta be the one to tell my story, like Fred MacMurray to
>the dictaphone in *Double Indemnity*.

And when I do, get the press in here right away, will ya, to publish
>the I.D. of the S.O.B.? Will ya do that for me, kid?

Awe 2

a moment surrounded in G-o-d
the beginning and end of A-ll-ah

Green

Look closely at one now. It is off-green,
asymmetrical. Another Design-
er, Who also doted on green, has been
changing much of His original to
off-green, too. As it was in the begin-
ning, it no longer is. But still, *The U-
nited States of America* is cen-
tered, wingspan stretching out to fill the line
right above His name, which is shared with the
rest of the Banker's Motto, ending: *WE
TRUST.* Is there blasphemy in the placement,
size, and choice of words (the creation of men,
after all)? The blatant asymmetry
and subtle color difference make it
more difficult today to counterfeit,
but what empire, what treasury, what mint
could have conceived of such a currency
and dream the billing were appropriate?

The Birth of Capitalism

For the first fifteen centuries
    of Christendom
the banning of banking
    and proscription of profit
made the merchants and bankers
    Muslims and Jews.
Did God in all His
    capitalistic glory
His new-age new-found wisdom
    whisper to a pope
to change the rules?

    —There's too much money
to be made. Sure, modest interest
    is allowed. Just not
usury, which is
    unreasonable and a sin.
—But Lord, does this mean
    Absolute Truth,
Thy Truth, is not eternal
    and immutable?
—No, Dumpkopf, the rule's
    always been
the same, it's your
    interpretations
down there, you so
    imperfect
exegetes and
    evangelists.
—Oh. I see. I guess.
    —And who
are you to question, you?
    —Right.

—And how about some
    golden statuary
to celebrate My glory?
    —Really?
But Jesus said—
    —And look what I did
to him, for spreading
    that cult of
humility.
    —Cult?
—It's glory Glory GLORY
    that I want.
Look at that first commandment.
    Fear Me. Worship Me!
Why do you think
    I sent you capitalism?
So you can make
    My temple
bigger than the next guy's
    and brighter, and
richer. And how
    can you obliterate
the infidel without
    brave armies and
technologies! —'*Tech-
    nologies?*'—Like
atom bombs. —*Adam who?*
    He had a last name?
—How'd I ever let you
    get elected Pope?
—*I'm not arguing, Lord.*
    I only want
to see. So, money?

                                —continued

  —Money! All
you can make for
  the glory of —*Yes
I know. God in the highest.*
  —Did you just interrupt
Me?
  (The pope sealed
his lips and threw
  away the key,
his eyes as big as
  silver dollars, or
golden ducats, rather.)
  —And don't bother
Me again. This magic lamp only
  gives me one more
visit, and you know
  what that one
has to be for.
  —*Oh!*
—So don't make me come down there again
  until it's time!

And thus we owe
  the growth if not
the birth of
  Capitalism
to the family-binding
  principle of
*Just wait till your Father
  gets home.*

Spire

A church's height will match a city's sins.
A church's height must match a city's sins.
A church's height should match a city's sins.
A church's height can't match a city's sins.

Cathedral steeples soar, therefore, but can
account for only half, and call it greatness.

marmorata

St. Peter's, The Vatican

    marmor marmor marmor
        clackle ackle ack
            scuffle squish scuffle uffle squeak
And myriads of modern feet
shod in modern ways
circulate in semi-stanchioned chaos
in general ungenuflective
randomly reflective
on centuries-buffed, unsentimental stone
red ropes keep them amply apart
      clackle ack
jackets, sweaters, sweatshirts
guarded over arms
draped over shoulders
tied around waists
might be forgotten but not like souls be lost
         marmor
assorted straps and cameras
slung unslung and slung
commemorate the singular occasion
           click
The multitude pounds lightly
their gasps and murmurs
soft and sweet, so they do not
drown out the omnipresent echo
the sanguine susurrations of the stone.
    marmor marmor marmor
What buried bishops whisper through the marble?
         marmor
What hard soles
tickle unread chiselings

now all but worn away
on coffin lids?
     clackle

What smaller-personed sneakers
in innocent abandon
impressed irrespective of the times
slide and scrape?
  squish
What agony or token
of what untamed apostle
is being
trampled on
only to resound
     uffle
in what artists' conglomerates of
what sundry styles that scream
out secrets through the silence of the stone
      marmor scuff
for a quarter hour's stroll
of a millennium?

  marmor marmor marmor
    clackle ackle ack
      scuffle squish scuffle uffle squeak

Chess and the Master

... And in this room I keep my prized,
one-of-a kind, hand-carved,
ivory and ebony ... Or was it onyx and jade?
I'm pretty sure, that is, that it was hand-made....

Shall we go in? It's right behind
the door if I recall
tucked in the corner.....

Perhaps it's under things.
Well, I thought that's where I'd put it.
Perhaps not.

The troops stand at attention,
on the checkered past of a battlefield
of the fabled age when kings wore robes
and knights rode steeds and queens almost flew
and soldiers were slain as if they didn't mind.

I'm sure we'll recognize it when we see it.
Pardon the dust, but it has been
a long time since I played.

Perhaps the other corner.

Ah, here they stand, still, poised—
why, in the middle of a game!
Whose move was it, do you recall?
Wait, I have to sneeze.
Or was it someone else
now that I think of it
who was playing?

Workshop Vision

When women met in woods, what rights and work
did they bespeak, what spells? or did they bow
to Nature, to the gods, or demigods?
And what experts' insignia did they wear?
We do not know; they left no trace, no laws.

Then when the mitred men in scarlet robes
like mortar'd scholars met in Anatolia
they handed down a workshop version of
what they'd proclaimed had been a word of God.

Later councils ramified for vainer
purposes like licenses to kill.

In England at the onset of her empire
other distorters drafted—crafted—a Tome,
the inconvenient, cut, like boring scenes.
What's left: two testaments to an island tongue
deployed as arms, dread as the sovereign's mace.

Today, in this selfsame language, across the world,
workshops convene and cackle, draped in accreditation
conferring, on some, degrees, on some, awards,
citations thick as prophylactic robes
unleashing workshop vision on the world.

What can we do athwart the hollow burgeoning?

O join me on a solstice up a mountain
in a wood where laws can't reach to tell us what
bright badge or clothes or anything to wear
nor peers approve permutings of our prose
where we can be as fearless as the wood.

The Margin of Error

You seem to have a vague recollection of an Old Friend you loved
Who hasn't kept in touch
but still you write
unsure of whether it's the right address
because you think you were close once—
or was it only once upon a time?
or in a previous life, at that?

You've tried to write the story of the former intimacy
and called it scripture, sometimes;
sometimes, myth.

And at the edge of an abyss we stand and think we hear
"Leap! Leap!" but cannot really be sure
and think it's that Old Friend
    but are not sure.
And yet we feel we have to do something,
and the trauma's so great
it splits our personality in two:

Science, which first susses out the terrain,
mapping more and more of *terra incognita*,
inventing seeing and listening devices to estimate the distances,
trying to figure out how to build
    a bridge across, a ladder down, a rocket up and over
so we won't have to leap so bloody far,
go splat unnecessarily;

Religion, resentful of these innovations,
says, "No, you have to jump from way back here,
    just like forever.
We cannot disappoint our Old Friend:
Running starts are not allowed."

And, once the head of the family and used to being right,
or making everyone think that he was right,
or say as much, at any rate,
he'll murder Science every now and then.

When all Science wants and warns is
"No, it's closer from up here!
Why guess and hope what you can know?"
Yes, Science combines the cleverness of Wile E. Coyote
    with the genius of the Road Runner, in one;
Religion, the gullibility of the one
with the impetuousness of the other.

Yet even Science hears the voice
    or thinks he hears a voice
and stands at an abyss
where the whistle in the wind,
the open spaces,
make him feel he too
must do something.

When Science thinks that in the end
he will not need Religion,
he thinks erroneously.
But usually it is Religion that fears Science, erroneously:
Both require the Artist as the Intrepid Arbiter;
Both require the same leap of faith.

The Evangelist

> *In the Beginning, the Gods . . .*
> —Genesis

"You have said one and have said three.
And Christ—is he alive or dead?
Which is it to be?" I said,
exposing the anomaly.
My evangelist, a childhood friend,
fired back, "He is *like* a person
with a changing personality."
"But does that strengthen or worsen
your exegesis, in the end?
I understand the clover leaf
analogy, but not the grief
imposed." I pointed out to her
the Hebrew word was *Elohim*
and *plural*. My evangelist
confirmed this with her minister;
then wept for all the evils done
to pagans in the name of One
when hers, too, was a Pantheon;
then she locked a door and sliced a wrist—
surviving, I am glad to say.

She used to rattle on and on
but now attempts to listen more
and rarely summons metaphor,
set speeches, or a preaching voice, today.
Of course I am relieved
that she survived.

Bridge

I see supports at either end.
The rest, though, is a riddle:
Why doesn't it begin to bend
or break, in the middle?

I've seen the diagrams that show,
with streams of numbered arrows,
where all its weight's *supposed* to go
instead of down the Narrows

but don't grasp engineering's quirks
and so feel overawed
with skepticism that it works,
suspicion of a God.

Sunday School

In front of the rows of hard, unsettling benches
suspended overhead
a troubled, tortured, giant man
was trying to writhe, but couldn't.
It wasn't his fault, I know, but the goriness
scared me half to death,
the way he hung there, indoors, but in the sky.
Dead or not dead, that was the question.
But no one would give a clear answer.
He was like the wood he was made from:
a living matter, alive no longer.
In Science I learned a good word for it:
organic.
Feeling nothing while feeling everything,
still growing, though done growing,
speaking, though he couldn't speak,
nailed down in his nakedness,
downcast while elevated,
lording over us even from his misery.
There was not just flesh and wood. There was red,
whether rust, or blood, or paint
I was too small to distinguish.
Miss Lane, the Sunday school teacher, said
it was beautiful. It was horrible.
I tried to get her to see that the man was dead.

But next to him, in a niche on the side,
a Lady held her arms out wide.
And outside, in the spring, the trees
grew leaves like the Lady's hair.
The Lady smiled. The Lady did not scare.

❖

I've long since outgrown Sunday school,
but I like the trees behind the church,
and still ride my bike there to play
on a sunny spring or summer day.

Come, take my hand. Now, touch a tree
with your other. Reach up. Patiently.
Ah. Notice how the gentlest breeze
lifts us as it lifts the trees.
Feel your fingers tremble and rise
and become the leaves, the breeze, the skies,
hanging, suspending us higher than
the treetops or any painted ceiling
and whatever naked organic man
might be stretched beneath—not kneeling
but on tiptoe, together, tall as the trees, feeling!

Grammar Lesson

The lesson—lessons—started in the fall—
or Fall—when Heaven moved, changed, and became.
Or heavens. In New England, with the sultry
hues of a slow motion fireworks display,
leaves folded, fell and started to turn in-
to mulch, but filled the air with their crisp sparks
of resilient, resplendent industry.

❖

When the die was first cast, dyes were cast too.
As lots were drawn, sides chosen, and teams formed,
no angel was destroyed in the making
of these—this—Cosmos. For as Cosmos is,
these cosmos are. And the heavens are Heaven.

❖

And "In the beginning" *they* called them E-
lohim—the Gods. Yes, the original
says "Elohim." Since then old deities
have been demoted to angels and saints
by man, but their divine nature remains
unchanged as the motto *e pluribus unum*.

❖

Likewise all Ocean's one, although there are
many seas, rivers, lakes, et cetera.
And "their" tides surge, smoothing edges, washing
borders like sins, eroding, replenishing,

instruments—instrument—of Shiva, both
healer and destroyer; of the Holy
Spirit, flame and dove, One of Three as One.

❖

As Life's all things living, and Cosmos all
things being, the distinction of number
is ours alone: it was never Theirs.

Buttress

From a bird's vantage point, the cathedral
looks like a many legged (if not winged) bug
stuck in the mire. You ask, What could be ug-
lier? The buttress is invisible,
though, from inside. And even gaudiness
can hold a godliness. All bugs are His,
after all, as what's in the stone walls is
a sanctuary like the soul of us,
that albatross which waddles, void of grace,
until it struts and flaps to gain the skies.
The buttresses hold everything in place
and make it safe for ambulatory eyes
to look up, dappled by the bleeding light,
and, if not fly, be humbled by the height.

Apples

It was too late for me. By age five,
I had gone apple picking with my family
and learned to like the picking and the apples,
all sorts. And autumn. And by age five I'd

grown curious about everything and was
told stories of what happened and I learned
things and liked knowing. Though I had not heard
of the story of the apple in the garden,

or the snake. And by age five I had myself
a pet snake I'd tell stories, and feed apples.
It preferred mice and wrapping around me tight
enough to tell me that it loved me, never

to cause alarm. It wasn't till age six
I learned about the garden and the apple
and the serpent. Which was too late because
I had already grown to like, and still

like, gardens—planting, tending, picking, eating—,
all sorts of weather, and autumn and winter,
and learning things and sharing what I know
with people of all sorts, and snakes and apples.

Desert-Ambling, or, The Beauty Part

The beauty part came later, that they'd heard
from their respective thrones about the birth
and set out, gilded, frankincense'd and myrrh'd
to kneel in dung as if the Kid was worth
it, lading Him with gold and gifts and *things*
like idiots—you know He'd chase out money changers, later. Now if they were kings
they needn't have been wise. But who sent word
that Joseph's wife was about to bear a Son?
Sure, she was House of David, but if expected,
why didn't they make sure that He was safe
in castle walls with doctors, not neglected
with hay for swaddling clothes, and no mid-wife?
And Caspar, Melchior, and Balthasar
went unnamed for eight centuries: bizarre,
considering the space in scripture spent
on naming names. Hmm. Could be when they started out, though. Sure—and here's the beauty part,
Part Two. They are still ambling, 'cause they are
still unaware they started out too late,
and wonder where the famous manger went,
three "Magi," magic travelers who reappear
as three mirages in a desert haze—
if not in Palestine, then down the street!—
still sure as ever that the site is near,
for us to hope they find, one of these days.

"Moses"

What happened to "Moses?" Although he died
right before reinvading promised lands,
he came back to the world transmogrified.
His spaceship crashed and plopped him on the sands,
recall, and he was made once more a slave,
this time by chimpanzees—that talked. And he
knew not where he was till he, ever brave,
escaped and found the corpse of Liberty
decapitated. Once he touted Ten
Good Rules, but what has happened to him since,
our chisel-chinned male lead, to twice escape—
with Israel, then with less warsome men—
only to preach of arms and violence,
still fearing the Egyptian, and the ape?

—Charlton Heston, 1923–2008

Interpretation

The Reverend Doctor hurled his epithets
like fire and brimstone from the very throne
of heaven, over all of us, his "pets,"
reminding us that we were not alone,

but being watched. One day he brought a book
with His picture in it to Thommie Meeks
(who rarely went to church) and made him look.
He'd dropped by Thommie's, Saturdays, for weeks.

Meeks was an orphan and a little slow,
but functional. His dad had been a friend
of Doctor Loud's. But Thommie didn't know
Loud's interest had a metaphysical end.

Next week the Doctor bought the boy a tie
and taught him how to tie all afternoon
while telling him over and over a whitish lie
to scare him: that he'd meet his Maker soon.

The note: "I'll be there Sunday, Rev. Loud.
Signed, Thommie Meeks. P. S. You see I tied
the thing myself. Thanks. Father will be proud."
Officials called the case a suicide.

At Thommie's services a tiny crowd
showed up: the Doctor, me, and an aunt, who cried.

Gothic

Its towers, stone antennae once, now rise
like giant swords flexed in an age of guns
and bombs, their potency wrung from traditions.
But as with the frilly and foppy guise

of a Swiss Guard, they serve their purpose, and
masses still swarm below. A shrill guide herds
twelve tourists past a wall of graven words,
which few can read, and fewer understand,

while graven figures do their best to scare:
wild demons, framing portals with despair,
and, higher, gargoyles pissing streams of grief.

The people do not look up from the square
but leave a greasy breadcrumb here and there
for pigeons, reveling in the relief.

Four Realms

    I. Philosophy—What

Figuring out
what cannot be
figured out
as if there were
somehow somewhere sometime something
worth figuring out?

    II. Science—How

Figuring out
what Someone else
has already figured out
so there might be more
to figure out
sometime?

    III. Religion—Why

Factoring in
what Someone's already
factored out
and factoring out
what Someone's already
factored in?

    IV. Poetry—And

Figuring in?
Perhaps.
Go figure.

David and Absalom

O Absalom! King David cried
and held the corpse, *My Absalom!*
When I read this tale I tried
my best not to cry.

I have a friend named Absalom.
His father was named David.
This Absalom has not been slain
but is a man. He now goes by
his middle name, David.
And when he had a son, he named
him Absalom.

Another friend, we called "Hay, Zeus!"
that's Jesus. He died young.
They said his father was alive
and not that far away,
when he didn't appear at the funeral.
Jesus died without a son
but many have been named for him
and many mothers hold him still
and dowse him with stone tears.

Oil Can

Some say God is The Oil Can; some, The Oil;
Some say The Mechanic who uses these;
Some say The Engineer whose craft and toil
Designed the thing to go, to work, to please,
As if He, like Gepetto, were A Man
In Wizened Years who chiseled company.
But now not just our joints could use The Can
But our hearts, too, to meet humanity.

Yet what can grease the squeaky gears of grace
And spirit? or should The Carpenter go
Back to re-work what lies behind the face,
Reconceive our capacity to know
That all that breathes is as sister and brother—
And learn to serve as oil can for each other?

Lamp Stand

I learned when I was six and Sundays went
to Sunday School as well as mass, that this,
when lit, was the eternal flame and meant
that He was present in His house, that church.
No sooner had I learned this magic lesson
one Sunday morning than the Saturday
that followed, at my first confession (this
the one time that I had to make up sins,
for looking down the list I feared that none
fit me and we were all required to go
but for the life of me and to this day
I could not think of any sins that day
and so I lied in the confessional,
made up all sorts of wild infractions that
the next week I'd have lies I could confess.
Which I did. But I'm ahead of myself) . . .
On this fall Saturday, the day that marks
the beginning of the end of the world
which every day since then has, too, I think,
I rode my bike down to St. Mary's, way
too early for confession, with my pal,
a Protestant named Harry, my best friend,
in fact. I figured I'd show him around
and at that time churches were never closed,
so I was told. What was I thinking then,
that I'd impress him, get him to convert
and save his soul? I don't think so;
I didn't learn till later who was damned
for not being a Catholic. I was six,
remember, and I think that what I thought
was everything about the place was cool,
and how much I too wanted to become

—continued

an altar boy when I was a big kid.
So down we biked and in we went, at 4—
confession was at 5—nobody there
but the huge doors were open, so I showed
him all around, the stations of the cross,
the vestry, and the altar where no boy
could set foot, ever, save the altar boys.
The walls pure white, the sunlight through the stained-
glass windows magic his church did not have.
Then I showed Harry how to dip his hand
in holy water, cross himself, and say
I'th'name and all. We waddled to the front,
where I then taught him how to genuflect
and kneel, and concentrate, hands clasped, and pray.
When I opened my eyes a scream came out
of me, for there, the flame of God was OFF!
Now this was the first crisis of my life—
the smallest and the largest, I believe.
Tear-drenched I shouted, FATHER! FATHER RYAN!
WHERE ARE YOU?! He appeared. *What's wrong, my son?*
HE'S GONE! *Who's gone?* GOD'S GONE! *What?* FATHER, LOOK!
And this I could not fathom at the time:
he smiled! *Never you worry. Who is this?*
I showed him Harry, unimpressed, I guess,
since he never did turn Catholic, but then who
would after this fiasco, at age six?
Then Father sent us off to play outside.
We rode our bikes around the parking lot.
It was a great, safe parking lot for that,
with tree clumps and the parish house to circle
around. No cars in the way. We had a ball.
And when the Catholics started to arrive
to expiate, Harry waited on the grass

as I went in to fabricate my faults
and sure enough, the flame had been restored
and never since then have I seen it off

till yesterday. I'd left the church at twelve,
remember, and I never did become
an altar boy—they did away with them
before I came of age—and since have learned
about such things as symbols, but to me
that flame was not the symbol *of*, it *was*.
So when I read in the *Globe* that my parish
was closing and would auction off its things
and Father Ryan had been sent to jail,
I went and won myself this gaudy lamp stand.
And it now stands here, in my entryway.
I bought the oil, too, and there's ample wick.

What do you think—light it, or leave it cold?

Patty Cake

	Mrs. Pendergast	swept through The Gate
to	meet her Maker and	meet her fate.
But	absolutely mortified by	who was there
she	pooh-poohed everybody	everywhere

so that

	in the end she came	out OK.
We	never did believe she was	going to stay.

God's Love

God's Love,
you say?
And Christ a Child of Love?
OK.
It's true.
That's why
today
us bastards smile and sigh
the way
we do.

I am Not That I Am

I am Not That I Am. What you are not.
I'm what might be. The other. Like the snake
called Nemesis, my fang thrills with a spot
of lubricant, a venom that you ache
to taste, or vice versa. I'm no mistake
of God but Nature's child, found in the brake,
the sky, your feet, your heart, your secret prayers,
your unvoiced breath, your second piece of cake.
The lesions of uncommon love affairs
gnawn knotty, unrequited. I'm the voice
of hissing thunder goading, the gadfly
of witty wisdom pointing out the choice
you face, convince yourself you'll never make,
who whispers in your gut to dream and try,
that thirst is something you're supposed to slake.
I hold a goblet to your lower lip
to show you how it's done, and smile. You sip
then grasp the glass and drown your reason. Why?
No reason. Simply, I am Not That I
Am, and I'm What You Want, and I'm nearby.

Divinity, or, Man

The holiest, wisest man still flawed,
I can't say which is worse:
creating, in his image, God,
or claiming the reverse?

Collection Basket

    It's not the same as when you passed
for 21 and had to buy Dad's booze,
    our howls and bruises then your last
concern. Now you are old enough to choose
    your charities, knowing what they
have done. And still you say you never knew?
    A miracle. You were away
that summer, and Dad fished with him, so you
    were not supposed to know. He's gone
now and can't make you give. I don't say grieve
    for me, only reflect upon
your contribution. Listen, and believe

        the cases worse than Gian and me,
        the altar boys who can't appear,
        the brothers' bruises you won't see,
            the screams you'll never hear.

Bakers

When we bake our own loaves, we use cultures of yeast
to effect the expansion of dough.
Small, invisible creatures that feast
on the sugars make everything grow.

But when they are baking, does the high heat
destroy the wee creatures, for bread?
I know bread that's risen is better to eat,
but feel somewhat sad for the dead.

So I mix my flour with molasses or honey,
far tastier than granules, I find.
Well it is their last meal. And I know that I'm funny
but can't help myself. Do you mind?

And I hope that The Baker will likewise be kind
and want to provide us a feast—
next time with enough oil or butter to bind—
and I hope we are more than His yeast.

Nature Walk

They brandish their pronouncements like cold swords.
My arms are air and water, glen and brook.
They castigate in King James English words
they've honed and, meeting me and sensing harm,
unsheathe, neglecting Nature's rounding arm.
I take them for a walk and let them look.

Sometimes a flick of water rusts their blade.
Sometimes the heated air turns swords to flames.
I sprinkle, pointing out a bush, a glade,
a leaning tree, a high supportive rock,
a heron. Most times nature walks don't work
at all. I take them for the other times.

Chimes

No chimes, no choir, no mourning rites;
No marble twelve feet tall;
For me they'll merely dim the lights
And silence may be all:

Or strike a rusted, tongueless bell
And crack it when I'm dead.
The pearly gates part just as well—
Better, some have said.

Potential

We do not know if God forgives.
We can't. When we recite
God saves, God loves, or *Jesus lives!*—
They may not, or They might.

We graceless mortals, though, can learn
to listen and adapt
to lessons, love our foes, and turn
the cheek that isn't slapped.

The Perfect Deity cannot;
Perfection is not learned.
So what we'll get is what we've got,
as far as He's concerned,

as great as He has always been,
and unsurpassed in love,
I'm sure. But we surpass Him in
potential to improve!

Not that I'm proud: Though man alone
enjoys this differential
of bettering himself, it's on-
ly difference in potential.

Few

You'd think the man who is undone
    by another man should call on God,
but mostly it's the other one.
    And few men note, or find it odd.

Easter 2003, A True Story

When the proselytizer approached
in the "wilderness"—well, I was on a bench
outside in a prairie state, so pretty close—
he rummaged through his snakeskin shoulder bag.
I said, *Nice bag. So whatcha selling, hm?*
—*Not selling anything. Here.* He showed me
a little magazine. I said *How much?*
—*Look first.* Pages of optical illusions
like games. *Things aren't what they seem.*
—*Like you seem to be selling but you're not.*
He wore a tie and looked about nineteen.
—*I'm giving. It's yours.* —*Thanks. And Happy Easter.*
—*Mind if I sit?* —*It's a public bench.*
I knew that it was coming now. And then
the pitch. —*I don't want money, just your soul.*
—*Oh, then you're buying, I figured as much.
Here, take it back.* —*Oh no, it's really yours.*
—*Not if you think I owe you anything.*
—*OK, OK!* —*I was just keeping the Sabbath.
Do you? The Sabbath?* —*What's that?*—*One day off.*
He didn't. *What other commandments don't you keep?*
I listed them for him. —*Surprised you don't
know them by heart, considering your line.
Of course, they're listed in a different order,
Leviticus from Deuteronomy.*
—*Are they?* —*You didn't know?* That's when he hit
me up for money. I explained to him,
*So you expect a contribution, then,
for the little magazine?* And he confessed.
*Well that's what we call selling in these parts,
and I already asked you if you were
selling anything. And you said no.
Remember, just 13 minutes ago?*

—I did. —That means that you're—. —Not what I seemed?
—Precisely what you seemed, except your need—
—To lie about it. —Wasn't necessary.
—So you think I'm a liar? —Doesn't matter
what I think, does it? If it bothers you,
that's good. —It doesn't. —Then that's bad. —Why so?
—Well, you brought up the Bible first, right? —Yes.
—You just had no idea that I was reading
one right now when you interrupted me
in meditations on an Easter morning,
did you? —No. I stopped there, picked up the Book,
and read. He asked what "story" I was on.
The Wilderness. Not Israel, the New
Testament. You know, the 40 days and nights?
The time the Devil reappeared to tempt?
Like today. —What? But—. —You don't agree?
I was just sitting contemplatively.
—What? —Didn't you, in truth, come up to me?

Religion 2: Not to Say

      The disbelief is chronic.
    But that is not to say I don't
enjoy a swig from time to time. So won't
        you pass around the tonic?

      I doubt it'll do any good, though.
    I know it's "filling and tastes great"
but that is not to say that it can sate
        the feeling that I should know

      more than liquory bubbles
    that bloat the paunch and spike the sense
with the faith I have abandoned ignorance,
        not to say, my troubles.

Bright Eye

A Bright Eye in the eastern sky
suspended in a nightly wink
changed the course of restless kings
by staying open, refusing to blink,
until they found the scene they sought
and craved. They'd left behind their things
and traveled light, in the cold and dark.
It showed which way to go and which way, not.

These stars leave me unsatisfied:
I keep on scanning for a spark
of such a brighter quality
to serve as beacon, flare, and guide
beyond the sequined galaxy.
You note the glimmers in my eyes:
They're only mirrors of the sky's
which gather dust and blink and wink
to be rinsed like suds in a vast black sink
but cannot take me anywhere
I crave to go—although I think
I'm happy, still and all, that they are there.

When the Collection Dish Comes Round

Pay the toll
before you're at
The Gate,
the fee
before the service
is required
and the soul
sets out—for what?
Then wait
to see
about The Furnace
being fired.

If lit,
don't get too close,
you might fall in;
if not
it gets too cold.
Nearby, a bin.
You'd buy a coal
but it
is not for sale!
And so you freeze
from spiritual
inconsistencies.

And then you wake. Relieved, you blink
so glad you haven't died,
not yet, then blink again to think,
Will coal then be denied
and warmth withheld for all you've prayed,
its rations based on—sin?
Has your allegiance been mislaid?—

but blink and give again
and pray they're based on what you've paid,
not on what you've been.

Feather and Flame

If you try to draw a flame
the scrawls and swirls invariably will
dovetail, fire being pennate in its form.
And just the exercise will make you feel warm.

One day, try this little game:
Tickle someone with a quill
on a palm or a foot, or under the chin.
Say you've lit a match there next to their skin.
Then when they open their eyes—
Surprise!

So rather than as a flame *or* dove,
He comes, when He comes, as a creature of
fire, safe flame and searing feather
at once, I'm moved to say. Whether
identified appropriately as,
or misattributed, He has
the vulture's timing, but will give
(as well as take) that all might live,
like The Bird That Burns, the phoenix. Or like Love.

Back Room

Some men call her by the nickname they dreamt up when she was young and a looker: Bliss.

But now her chest's uneven, one boob gone, the other repaired, her teeth that are left have turned brown, and she wafts pungent. . . . Well she doesn't douche as religiously now.

She parks it by a table in the rear, the customer comes up and pays his Washington, Hamilton or Franklin, and she lays him in the back room.

One or two are from the old days, they remember what they used to call her, but once I asked her her real name.

Oh yea, I said. I'd forgotten that she'd told me years ago, when I was young.

I asked her which she'd prefer. *Prefer for what?* she said. *For me to call you.* —*Oh, Honey, it don't matter. Faith is just a name. Whatever you call me, you know what I am.*

The Parson

Well the Parson tried
but then I died—
rather, lingered at the Crossroads. But
he barely cried

so they sent me back
through a magic crack
to save the burnished soul of that
man in black.

So I told him jokes
and I offered tokes
but he wouldn't share the peace pipe or
relax with folks.

In a burst of pride
he burst, and died.
So I waited at the Crossroads but
he landed wide.

(O I hope he'll never know that
no one cried.)

"The Creation of Adam"

If you stand underneath, face up and spin
A second—safely, for the Chapel's dim—
Then blink and open your eyes, but open
Truly to all the potential meaning
In the name "The Creation of Adam,"
You too might gather, in a sudden glimpse,
The other, the creation of *Adam's:*
One indexed downward and creating him;
He half-asleep, flexed up, imagining.

At the Center

At the center of the cross, the circle: Heart
which has been stilled in stone but not in death.
    The circle's center is the part
where nothing is, the lungs' insides, the breath.

The masonry's precise in either case
especially all over Ireland,
    though worn away in many a place.
There, cross and circle wed, embrace, and stand

as one at graves and sacred sites, like sages,
abstract executions wrought to give
    their mystic lessons from the ages
on how to die as well as how to live.

Circle and Cross

The cross and circle, which have been at odds,
are joined as one in Ireland. The cross
stands like a man and points outward four ways.
The circle floats: the world, the sky, the days,
the universe; it points no ways or all
ways, in as well as out. It's the Great Wheel.
The cross also suggests a sword or knife;
the circle, as you know, the Ring of Life.
And the circle makes the cross's heart
in Ireland; elsewhere, they're kept apart.

The Christ figure in many of Ireland's
churches is still alive and reaching out-
ward in a semicircle which, without
us, will stay incomplete. See how He stands
in stillness? It's a stillness that's a shout
to us to round Him out, by joining hands.

Out with Bacchus

Out with Bacchus, down with Baal,
    Ishtar's dead as night must fall.
Isis and Osiris, too,
    All of them no longer true.

Amon, Zeus and Jupiter,
    Mother Earth—who heard of her?
Ra Ra Rah—o what's the use?
    Even Jesus looks like Zeus.

Jehovah, Elohim, Yahweh,
    All of them have had their day.
Deities aren't meant to stay.
    Our money's on the USA.

Lesson from the Master

The more I grasped the Master's size,
deluded I could ever see
Him/Her through antiseptic eyes,
the more I was convinced She/He

was the Master of Humility,
kowtowing us with rim-starred skies,
an ocean's savage mystery. . . .
God—awed, and made the humble, wise.

But, meeting you, I realize
the rule divine of beasts and plants:
only what perishes, enchants;
and only with cherishing comes renew-
al; He/She's Dancing Master, too,
and would that we clasp hands, and dance.

The Reformed

Listen to their yelling.
See their perspiration.
    What the bejeepers are they selling
in such desperation?

Other roués have reformed:
Augustine, and Paul.
    But I just came in to get warmed
up, not to rock the hall.

Are they spurred by love or hate?
Sounds like they confuse
    the two. No, I cannot forget
all the past abuse.

And what about the reprobate
sitting in the pews
    who has not reformed quite yet
and still is on the loose?

Well the preacher's words weren't pretty
but we've had our snooze.
    Isn't it a goldarned pity
he can't hold his booze?

The Histories, Back When

The histories, back when, were only oral
so only those with ample memories
knew them. And though there might have been a moral,
it was built in, and for the centuries.
Well anyway those ancient histories
got written down at last. Then edited,
editorialized, translated,
redacted, deleted, parts selected
and argued—without the whole being read—
for vain concerns, alarming to the dead.

A preacher with a karaoke machine
in the Millennium Bar lights into his routine.
A stranger asks how he knows what it means.
Well who the hail are you, the preacher poses.
Let's say where I hail from they call me Moses,
the stranger says. The preacher talks and talks
till Moses grabs the karaoke box
and hurls it, smashing it to smithereens.

Religion 3: He stood draped

He stood draped to the nines and sang and doled
out magic in white wafers from a gold
cup. Brass, in fact. He said Take This And Eat
and as I took I felt both warm and cold
at once. Strange high—and low. I couldn't get
enough of it. But when I brought a friend
she asked me, "Are you sure he washed his hands?
And I'm not sure I like the way he stands."
And that was the beginning of the end.

I still go, now and then, and hear a lecture,
but from the back row, far more circumspect
of white things to be swallowed down with scripture
and rote. Old friends call me a "part-time fixture"—
though certain rites I find I can't reject
and, entering or leaving, genuflect.

Night Sky

You can see them in the night sky, all the warnings.
Some even linger late until the mornings.
But men dream God will send another Word—
While She's been screaming to be seen, and heard.

Heaven, Whateveritis

The moderns and postmoderns which
like big bad cats unravel the Whateveristhe Ball
to splay it out uneven to the core
excite to a postpostpostmodern thrall,
no hope, no heaven, no nothing anymore.
But if it's so that LIFE'S A B--CH
AND THEN YOU DIE, as tee-shirts tell
us and so many things so many sell,

will there not then be solace in the abyss,
an end of aches in the Whateveristhe Nothingness?
Maybe. Meanwhile I knead with other paws,
directed inwards, tamping but with claws
still unclipped, painful as analysis;
and through the process feel I've gained a purse
as sudden as an ached-for kiss
easing the Whateveristhe universe.

Saturdays

On Saturdays I would confess,
and Sundays, never miss a mass.
Now my mortal sins seem less.
    The venial, I let pass.

Now Saturdays I drive my son
to lend some good to a darkened life—
not for fear of what he's done
    but of my ex-wife.

And since a Cheshire cat must smile—
and go feral, if left alone—
I go in and pray awhile,
    and as chaperone.

Fear and Faith, An Interview

The way I see it, it's devils what rush in
where the faithful, wise or foolish, fear to go,
so a little faith and fear are probably
a good thing and I'm bringing 'em to you
to learn 'em right behavior, scripture, sin
and God. Too late for me. Besides I know
too much and have a job, best forget me.
Chopping down trees. Well it's something to do,
it puts food on the table. Gotta tell
you though, my babies never learned to lie.
So tell 'em what you will from out the Book,
and show 'em verse and chapter. They read well.
But if I see 'em so much as bat an eye
about, or come home with a funny look—
I guess it wouldn't be right polite to say
but I read about what's going on today
in Massachusetts and New Mexico.
That cardinal stepping down? You know? Good. So
best keep both faith and fear in these two facts:
I love my children, and I own an axe.

Organs

Munitions in the magazine
are quieter now than these
which summon legions to convene
for hymns and homilies.

But stockpiles grow in guns and souls
which while they are unheard
get catalogued like arsenals
waiting for the Word.

The preacher has the people come
for service to take pause
then, pulling out all stops for some
emergent, current cause,

keeps them ready to enlist
with arms to charge and fire
like plastic keys the organist
tickles to inspire.

Holidays

We've two for War: to decorate the dead
is one; the one for Veterans, the other.

For Jesus, three: birth, death, and back from dead.

Did everyone forget about His mother?

Revisions

Lao Tzu, Thoreau and Dr. King were jailed. But though they're dead,
people still know and even sing a lot of what they said.

King was killed. And Christ. And we have made them holidays.
The others willed us poetry to tell us of their ways.

Rosa Parks declined the seat her driver said to take.
For Joan of Ark's trailblazing feat they did her at the stake.

They are not quite holidays but have been canonized:
The future's got a lot of ways to see the past revised.

We hold the keys to our own star, but not who'll spin our story
in centuries, and if we are deserving of our glory.

King and Lao-Tzu died gloriously; but will the years be fair?
I wonder who they'll make of me: their jailer, or their heir?

The Exercise of Reason

Patrick reasoned unreasonably to show the 3-in-1 dogma
        through natural phenomena, with the shamrock analogy.
But when shown a four-leaf clover why didn't he do it over?
Pothos, poplars, and aspen trees also prove the properties of
        e pluribus unum, all conjoined at roots invisibly or,
        even more mysteriously, genetically identical;
while atomies and laser beams, once thought visionaries' dreams,
        spread like fire—the Holy Ghost—
or love, or even life, almost.

In the beginning were more than Him;
the noun first used in Genesis was plural, namely, *elohim*.
"I Am That I Am?"—They Are what He Is!
In spite of who decline to hear it, the Single Light, as Soul and Spirit,
        is not curtailed at Trinity but multiplies beyond
            the One into a blessed Pantheon expanding to infinity
            not subject to restraint—

while Patrick is no longer even Saint.

Postcard from *Republicca*

on the reverse, the image of Bernini's Ecstasy of St. Theresa *at Santa Maria della Vittoria, Rome*

The pillars stand as so many trees
turned to marblestone to attend her
and guide me along their alabaster path.
There she is frozen up on the wall
of her dimlit chapel to the side in the deep
of an enchanted, echoing, illustrated
forest, stuck forever, discovered
in her moment of being attacked by a wild,
loving angel, her writhing, her embarrassment,
her glee, her glory, suspended forever,

just off the *Piazza della Republicca*

where, as the belltower chimes every midnight,
families, cafés and *Eh Cumpari* bands transform
to the circus of a red light district,
the spell as regular as Cinderella's.
Without the angels, and with flesh in lieu
of marblestone, and with cars, horns,
colored lights and catcalls standing for
the guiding alabaster, one is led to
an ecstasy and holiness no statue
can know but as a dimlit memory,

or voyeur's faithful interpretation.

The Outlaw

was safe, behind the altar. There
no believer dared touch him, due to the
divine rule of sanctuary. And
everyone in town back then was a
believer. And acolytes brought him
a palette, and food and clothes, over
the years. But then came
the heathen invasion, and the conversion of
the church into a civic building, during which
he vanished, and—Well, here is where
the traditions veer. One says he was
martyred in the faith; another, he
escaped; the third, that he changed his
name and rules the secular
democracy even to this day.

Were He to think of sky

Were He to think of sky as land
and of land, not as land, but sea;
and of every sea as a cauldron of sky
where quickened creations don't swim, but fly:
what would He think of me?

Since fish, with neither foot nor hand
nor wing, can only swim,
must the sea worm that sees from below them call
them birds? And will eagles appear to crawl
when we sit next to Him?

Feathers 2

Time after time I want to do what's right,
but do what's common and popular
instead. Then in my dreams, I'm tickled by the slight-
est breeze, and shudder. It's as if it were

Good sailing by, as feathers in the mind
on a bird of intention, tacit and light,
or Virtue paddling past through the mire of night,
till she's swallowed by the darkness, leaving me behind.

From the dark of my dream, I can hear her caw,
though she wants to croon and coo. How she'd like to land
on the limb of a lilac, or a shoulder, and awe
with a tune, or a dance, so I'd understand

her, but, fearing my worst, she has stayed in flight,
dropping feathers now and then, soft and white.
I've seen them on the ground, engirding a stump,
and in the opening of a film. (Was it *Forrest Gump?*)

Last night I was out and was sure I heard
(though I thought I had imagined it) a sudden thump.
On the sidewalk, at my feet, there appeared this clump,
like a bundle of hope: a fallen bird.

Glad

Be glad I'm not a god, for if I were,
imagine the ennui you would incur.

In the age of the Pharaoh, if I were God
and you needed me, I'd be off erecting
a tomb: so you'd be glad that I was not.

In the epoch of conquerors, I'd be designing
a causeway to march my winged troops
over. In the era of emperors and popes

I'd be filling niches with art and stuff.
In the time of kings, I'd be on
a crusade, or, off-season, a hunting junket.

But if I were God today and you had
to talk you'd do best to show up on
the links Friday at noon. How's your golf?

And aren't you glad?

Exegesis on a Church Sign

I passed a church in Maryland today. It bore a sign
That said "Child Development Center." With that simple line
I realized what heretofore I'd failed to understand:

For instance, why they make statues and cathedrals so grand,
Enlisting glitter, gold and the majestic to deceive.
As bright-bowed boxes Christmas morning make a tot believe
In Santa Claus, the north pole, Rudolph's nose, and other merry tales,
They dress up scripture's sagas that we soak them up like fairy tales:
An archangel—a plot device like a fairy godmother;
Mary is Cinderella; her prince Charming—why, no other
Than You-Know-Who. And she was by no means the only one.
Recall the "voice" instructing Abraham to slay his son?
Bad fathers permeate both Charles Perrault and the Brothers Grimm.
Appalled by ours, or neighbors', we transfer our faith to Him.
Dear Daniel in the lion's den, and Jonah in the whale,
And Noah in his ark, all make a thrilling nursery tale.
(But I would like to think that there is a similar glory
In Aesop's Fables, or a Rudyard Kipling Just-So Story.)
Since children like their animals, the Bible is a zoo;
Kids naturally root for ugly duckling, underdog, and Jew:
I've always thought they had, referring to that parting Sea,
The chase-scene of all chase-scenes—or I did when I was three.
That Moses with his magic staff was cool when I was six,
And even eight- or nine- or ten-year-olds like magic tricks.
The horde fed with one loaf evokes a tale already known;
Have you not heard about how to make soup out of a stone?
The one who cured the lame and leprous might be a magician;
Today, though, we would label such a fellow a "physician."
It all depends on how they tell the story, and on when
They get to you. They don't wait till you're eight or nine or ten,
But start you off before the age of reason, which is seven.

That's when they tempt—yes, tempt—you with those overtures of heaven.
They scare the living daylights out of little kids with hell;
The teen-aged know it all, and it would be a harder sell.

To take a good hard look at dogma, doctrine, and church laws,
The details are perverse enough to give a grown-up pause.
How can an institution fault adulterer and bigamist
When all its Brides of Christ make Jesus himself a polygamist?
If any other woman were to amble down the aisle
For a groom long dead and gone, why, she'd be a necrophile.
And transubstantiation makes communion weird and bannable.
To eat the body, drink the blood?—A worshiper's a cannibal
Or vampire. And what flaw had the indomitable Divinity
That they had to reduce and codify It into Trinity?
I feel a shiver and confess I really would have rather
Not realized this makes the holy Infant his own Father.
Scenarios like this one are as unsettling a thing
As *Chinatown* (the movie) or a tale from Stephen King.
You know the kind of read I mean: you have to get your fill,
So turn the page, race to the end, although it makes you ill.
And then you read another one! With adventures this sick,
This lurid, violent, gory—Someone oughta make a flick.
Like, of the life of Moses—maybe make it animated.
(Take out the blood and sex, though, if you want it General-rated.)
Or take a coupla stories, turn them into music-theater—
Like Joseph and his motley robe—for kids. What could be sweeter
Than children humming all those tunes in popular pastiche:
The Pharaoh's Elvis Presley—oh the faith it will unleash!
King Herod?—Charlestons! Judas?—heavy metal!—oh, that's rich.
Let's make JC a superstar of rock 'n' roll and kitsch.

—continued

I know that I digress: here, it was not the Church per se,
But nonetheless, the entertainment world did find a way
To sell and spread the scripture to more youth and common folk,
Not unlike changing Latin to the English England spoke,
Deleting what they didn't like. Did not King James distill
The Story to his own ends, like Lloyd Webber and De Mille?
Those English academes and clerics, though, had the audacity
To say that what they wrote had theological veracity.
Episcopalian people—please. How can you give the nod
To words of James the First that claim to be the word of God?
That ersatz Anglican religion's managed to succeed
By using Bible passages to teach their kids to read.
Meanwhile, to counteract this populist interpretation,
In Italy and Spain they had this Counter-Reformation,
Where images of agony by Caravaggio
Made martyrs' lives as dark (and light) as Edgar Allan Poe.
The artists were inspired by guilt-inducing works of sages,
But really, it had been that way throughout the Middle Ages.
No wonder, then, that pope commissioned Michelangelo
To do it all again, and give the world a better show.
Today, with all its treasures and St. Peter's magic dome,
The Vatican's a theme park (have you ever been to Rome?).
Perhaps some purpose lies in this commandment I once read:
No graven image of God or creature AT ALL, it said.
I now see what this long-lost commandment might have been for.
(The Byzantines, beset by this one, even went to war.)
But a big bloody crucifix instills awe and respect;
A corpse makes sinners—and children—more apt to genuflect.

Don't think that I intended to make this verse a receptacle
For points of view cantankerous, irreverent, or skeptical.
It's just that when I saw that sign in Maryland, the dark

That seemed to have been imprisoning me, yielded to a spark
Of something new—a small idea, no "bath of mystic light" here.
For once, though, I began to think Karl Marx was almost right here.
With pageant and parade you can appease the lower classes;
By making them believe, you keep them disenfranchised masses.
It isn't just the current church, though: rulers throughout history
Have subjugated subjects by distracting from the Mystery.
So politicians, popes and princes find a way to work us
Not too unlike the way the Romans did with bread and circus.
The truth might be there right in front of us, but all the smoke
And mirrors make the merest introspective act a joke.

One Harvey Cox once said that in the West we are less able
To seek spiritual contents, tending more to read the label.
That's why so many have turned East; with Paradox one can
Begin to break away and start to grasp the soul of man.
But don't Christ's parables integrate the West with the East?
His cryptic comments puzzle and provoke, to say the least.
So is the Church, core and affect, a Child Development Center
And voluntary prison, too? Or might it serve as mentor
To one or two who'll ponder points too hard to understand
In groups of more than one or two? Could it be that they planned
To lure the folks with festival, first get us in the door
And then invite the few with a glimmer of something more?
And does God care, as long as you follow the Golden Rule?
Does contemplative wisdom beat the blind faith of a fool?
And I am one to talk: Have you noticed this exegesis
Does not illuminate a thing? Though, since I hope it pleases,
The prosecutor's guilty of an irony sublime:
To lure and then distract you, I've set the thing in rhyme.

A Certain Faith

The kind of faith that I'm
    talking about
is not the kind that you
    can talk about.
It isn't faith in time
    or space or ex-
istence, or God, or you,
    or love or sex—
Though these latter ensue
    from what I am
trying to refer to:
    It's of the gram.
Of the electron. The
    suspicion of
the neutron. And the be-
    lief (so like love
but firmer and faster
    than anything
human) of the master
    proton (sitting
while electrons spin) in
    electrons and neu-
trons, and in a proton
    elsewhere. Or two.
In a gazillion.
    Never mind Who,
What, Where, Why,
    How or When.
An atom, saint or sin-
    ner, can DO.
Likewise, I note my skin
    has succeeded
in holding me within,

and I'm not dead. . . .
Yet! Such a faith is true faith,
    unshakeable,
a faith far worse than Death—
    better than All.

And all that All

And all that All
    has ever been:
the junkyard dog
    chained out in back

with just enough give
    on his leash to make
him proud to think
    he catches his own food.

Litany

Is all this acting up then
but our adolescent efforts
to try to get an avuncular, gadding Father
to turn His Head for once
even if it's to smack us a Good One?

And if so good that the smiting slays
then at least we know we got His goat,
that the Whole Thing hasn't been for naught
and should we get to meet Him, we'll
be able to say We won! We won! We—

Which we won't, of course, but simply
knowing we can might be enough
for us to be able to cope with this
inferiority complex, make forever almost bearable.

Face to Face, A True Story

I saw God face to face today
And was not even dead.
He told me that He was a She
As well. I understood.

She then said, "He, She, It or They:
Whichever you prefer,
For We're beyond the scope of We,
Us, They, Them, Him, or Her."

I rifled through my Holy Book,
Then heard The Voice again.
It whispered, "Let Us have a look,"
As if They'd never seen

The Thing! She didn't have to say,
For in a flash, I knew—
Divinely—telepathically:
What I'd believed was True

Was otherwise. Nor find it odd
Men use *He* all they can
When chiming not the Word of God,
But the words of man.

The Moment

The moment of God
deciding to violate a virgin
as so many of his Colleagues had once done
might seem a salient episode
for a terrific turmoil-stuffed Role
in some deep and daring drama
hallowing and harrowing the times.

A human, mortal and flawed,
to conceive of such a Character
would border blasphemy, as
so many worthwhile words
so duly dare.

The human role, however, as per usual,
proved far more piquant, poignant, and perplexing.
For what dim-witted power-hungry person
should ever espouse a God that sires by force,
and such an awe-full act
part of a Plan?

Not What You Might Think

God is
not what or Who
God is

because
of your
belief.

God does
what and to whom
God does

in spite
of your
disbelief.

To Help You Think

To help you think of God, think of tomorrow.
Or vice versa. Tomorrow can't be seen
or held, tomorrow does not weigh, and yet
you know tomorrow's always coming. But
tomorrow, once it does arrive, is gone.
Tomorrow's never here, is never now,
and yet tomorrow is responsible
for (very nearly) Everything. And any
depiction can be only science fiction.

To help you think of God, think next of love,
or vice versa, which is the way tomorrow
comes to us as with a kiss, or
the eternal hope thereof—that is tomorrow.
That is God. That's love. Like hope. Like thought.

Acknowledgments

Grateful acknowledgment is made to the editors of the following publications and websites where these poems first appeared:

The Abstract Elephant: "Nature Walk"; *Alabama Literary Review:* "So, The Modern"; *Ancient Paths:* "At the Center," "Desert-Ambling, or, The Beauty Part," "Oil Can," and "To Help You Think"; *Aries:* "Bakers" and "Kinds"; *The Aurorean:* "Checking"; *Avocet:* "The Belfry"; *Blue Unicorn:* "Acts of Creation," "The Exercise of Reason," and "Holidays"; *California Quarterly:* "Thriller"; *cc&d:* "Back Room," "The Birth of Capitalism," and "Chess and the Master"; *Clackamas Literary Review:* "Chimes" and "Interpretation"; *Concho River Review:* "Shortcoming"; *The Dark Ones: Tales and Poems of the Shadow Gods* (Bibliotheca Alexandrina): "Above and Below" and "Confusion 1"; *enskyment* (Moon Shadow Sanctuary Press): "Feather and Flame"; *Fickle Muses:* "Hellsgate"; *Ginosko:* "The Moment in a Service"; *Harbinger Asylum:* "Easter 2003, A True Story" and "The Evangelist"; *Home Planet News:* "One Day Years Ago" and "The Moment"; *Istanbul Review:* "If each star"; *Italian Americana:* "Cathedrals" and "The Creation of Adam"; *IthacaLit:* "Religion 1: The teller emerges"; *Literary Hatchet:* "Hell," "Litany," "Out with Bacchus," "Religion 2: Not to Say," and "Saturdays"; *Lord of the Horizon: A Devotional Anthology in Honor of Horus* (Bibliotheca Alexandrina): "Beatitudes and Bravery"; *Mastodon Dentist:* "Sunday School"; *mgversion2>datura:* "Blade"; *Mission at Tenth:* "Lamp Stand"; *Muddy River Poetry Review:* "And all that All" and "Postcard from *Republicca*"; *Out of Nothing: Poems of Art and Artists* (Shanti Arts): "Gothic"; *Ovunque Siamo:* "Alternate Perspectives"; *Pacific Review:* "The Outlaw"; *The Purpled Nail:* "Mixed Praise"; *Quickening: Poems from Before and Beyond* (Cyberwit.net): "Heaven, Whateveritis"; *The Recusant:* "Heraclitus" and "marmorata"; *The Road Not Taken:* "Religion 3:

He stood draped"; *The Same:* "After Eve"; *Sewanee Theological Review:* "Bridge"; *Showbear Family Circus:* a previous version of "Revisions"; *Southwest Review:* "Buttress"; *Steam Ticket:* "Four Realms"; *Stickman Review:* "Potential"; *Studio One:* "Bright Eye"; *Sunken Lines:* "I am Not That I Am"; *Texas Review:* "Crèche"; *Toe Tree Journal:* "If you think you see God by day"; *U.S. 1 Worksheets:* "Apples"; *Verse Wisconsin:* "Fear and Faith, An Interview"; *VIA:* "Collection Basket" and "Spire"; *Word Gumbo:* "The Process of Water"; *Wordland:* "Night Sky" and "One time, in the middle"

About the Author

James B. Nicola is the author of five collections of poetry. His decades of working in the theater as a stage director, composer, lyricist, playwright, and acting teacher culminated in the nonfiction book *Playing the Audience: The Practical Guide to Live Performance*, which won a *Choice* award.

Shanti Arts

Nature • Art • Spirit

Please visit us online
to browse our entire book catalog,
including poetry collections and fiction,
books on travel, nature, healing, art,
photography, and more.

Also take a look at our highly
regarded art and literary journal,
Still Point Arts Quarterly, which
may be downloaded for free.

www.shantiarts.com

www.ingramcontent.com/pod-product-compliance
Lightning Source LLC
LaVergne TN
LVHW041337080426
835512LV00006B/503